SHOCKING STORIES • AMA RECO... • STATS

THE ULTIMATE BASEBALL FACTS BOOK

FOR KIDS

Broadwood Press are an independent publishing team that aims to provide fun and educational books for young readers.

All facts within this book are accurate at the time of publishing. However, if you happen to spot anything that needs to be corrected, **please email us at broadwoodpress@gmail.com** and we will be more than happy to help you out.

ISBN: 9798345699034

1.

Baseball became popular in the United States during the 1800s.

2.

Soldiers used to play baseball to pass the time, so it quickly became known as 'America's Pastime.'

3.

The first official baseball game took place in 1846, in New Jersey.

4.

The game was won by the 'New York Nine' who beat the 'Knickerbockers' 23-1.

5.

The modern rules of baseball were developed by a man named Alexander Cartwright.

6.

As well as being a baseball fanatic, Alexander Cartwright was also a firefighter.

7.

The Cincinnati Red Stockings were the first-ever official baseball team.

8.

They became an official team in 1869.

9.

Seven years later, in 1876, the National League was founded.

10.

The National League is the oldest professional sports league that still exists.

11.

The National League makes up one half of the MLB.

12.

The other half is made up of the American League which was founded in 1901.

13.

Baseball was inspired by older bat and ball games like rounders and cricket.

14.

The World Series began in 1903 and is one of baseball's main competitions.

15.

The New York Yankees have won more world series titles than any other team.

16.

Jack Robinson made history in 1947 when he became the first black baseball player.

17.

The time period 1900-1920 is known as the 'dead ball era'.

18.

This is because not many home runs were scored during this time.

19.

During the dead ball era, teams averaged only 3.4 runs per game.

20.

However, by 1921, teams were hitting four times as many home runs than they were in 1918.

21.

Despite a lot of research, baseball historians still don't know what caused the dead ball era.

22.

Some suggest it was the introduction of the foul strike rule and some believe it was due to the size of the stadiums/parks.

23.

Babe Ruth is one of baseball's most famous players and contributed to the end of the dead ball era.

24.

This was because he introduced an aggressive style of batting that other players copied.

25.

The first modern farm system was developed in the late 1920s and early 1930s.

26.

It was developed by Branch Rickey, who invested in minor-league clubs.

27.

Little League Baseball was founded in 1939.

28.

Sadly, many minor-league teams broke up due to player shortages as a result of World War II.

29.

Despite being known for his aggressive batting, Babe Ruth doesn't hold the record for the most home runs scored.

30.

The record is held by Barry Bonds who hit 762 (48 more than Babe Ruth).

31.

Despite this, Barry Bonds is not in the National Baseball Hall of Fame.

32.

Lou Gehrig was known as 'The Iron Horse.'

33.

He got this nickname due to his ability to continue playing, despite being injured.

34.

On top of this, he played over 2,100 matches in a row.

35.

Gehrig played in the All-Star Game seven times in a row and won the American League MVP twice.

36.

In 1939, Lou Gehrig was elected into the National Baseball Hall of Fame.

37.

More than 900,000 baseballs are used in an MLB season.

38.

Willie Mays is credited with the greatest catch in the history of baseball.

39.

This play became known as 'The Catch' and took place on September 29, 1954.

40.

In 1887, softball was invented as a winter version of baseball.

41.

At the time, it was simply known as 'indoor baseball' or 'indoor-outdoor.'

42.

Joe DiMaggio holds the record for the most hits in consecutive games.

43.

Between May 15 and July 17, 1941, he recorded hits in 56 consecutive games.

44.

Nolan Ryan threw more than 5,700 strikeouts during his career.

45.

He still holds the record for the most strikeouts in a baseball career.

46.

Barry Bonds holds the record for the most home runs in a single season.

47.

In 2001, he hit 73 home runs while playing for the San Francisco Giants.

48.

The American major leagues didn't include a Canadian team until 1969.

49.

The first Canadian team to join was the Montreal Expos, joining the National League.

50.

In 1977, the Toronto Blue Jays joined the American League.

51.

In 1847, baseball was officially played in Mexico for the first time.

52.

The first official baseball league outside of the US and Canada was founded in Cuba, in 1878.

53.

The English soccer team Aston Villa were the first winners of the National League of Baseball of Great Britain.

54.

The European Baseball Confederation (EBC), was founded in 1953.

55.

The EBC is responsible for organizing games between teams from different countries.

56.

Baseball was first introduced as an Olympic medal sport in 1992.

57.

However, it was removed from the Olympics for the 2012 games.

58.

A big reason for its removal was that MLB was against players competing during a major league season.

59.

Instead, the World Baseball Classic was introduced to act as a high-profile international tournament.

60.

A 'fastball' is the fastest type of pitch in baseball.

61.

It is also the most common type of pitch thrown in baseball.

62.

Fastball pitches can often exceed 100mph (160kmh).

63.

Fastballs are thrown with backspin, which causes the ball to move upward.

64.

The scientific name for this upward movement is the 'Magnus Effect.'

65.

MLB recognizes three different types of fastball: The four-seam fastball, the two-seam fastball and the cut fastball.

66.

The four-seam fastball is the most common of the three.

67.

The two-seam fastball is also known as a 'Sinker', due to its downward movement.

68.

The cut fastball is also known as the 'Cutter.'

69.

The cut fastball is slower than the four-seam fastball but it creates a lot more movement.

70.

The fastest MLB pitch ever is 105.8mph (170.2kmh). It was a four-seam fastball.

71.

The pitch was thrown by Aroldis Chapman on September 24, 2010.

72.

The average four-seam fastball has increased by 2mph (3kmh) since 2008.

73.

In 2008, only 214 fastballs were recorded at over 100mph (160kmh).

74.

By 2023, the number of fastballs reaching more than 100 mph (160kmh) had increased to over 3,800.

75.

This increase in speed has also led to an increase in arm-related injuries.

76.

A breaking ball is a pitch that moves to confuse the batter.

77.

The slider, curveball and screwball are all types of breaking ball.

78.

The slider is one of the fastest breaking balls, averaging between 80mph (130kmh) and 90mph (140kmh).

79.

The slider causes the ball to move towards the pitcher's glove side.

80.
Players under the age of 13 are discouraged from throwing sliders as they can easily cause injury.

81.
A 12-6 curveball is a type of pitch that causes the ball to dip as it approaches the batter.

82.
Its unpredictable nature is where the phrase 'to throw a curveball' comes from.

83.
The average MLB curveball has a velocity of 77mph (124kmh)

84.

Curveballs are also not recommended for young kids due to the high risk of injury.

85.

A 12-6 curveball gets its name from the movement of the ball being like the hands on a clock at 12 and 6.

86.

Candy Cummings is thought to have invented the curveball.

87.

A screwball moves in the opposite direction to a curveball or slider.

88.
A screwball is also known as an 'airbender' or 'scroogie.'

89.
Carl Hubbell was known as the 'scroogie king' because he threw so many screwballs.

90.
The 'changeup' is a pitch thrown to look like a fastball, but is in fact, a lot slower.

91.
A changeup is roughly 8-15mph (13-24kmh) slower than a regular fastball.

92.

A changeup is so effective because the human eye can't detect it until it is 30 feet (9 metres) away.

93.

A 'knuckleball' is a pitch that has very little spin and is unpredictable.

94.

Out-of-the-park home runs are a lot more common than inside-the-park home runs.

95.

A grand slam is when a home run is achieved with all the bases loaded.

96.

In April 1999, Fernando Tatis hit two grand slams in one inning.

97.

In August 2011, the New York Yankees became the first team to hit three grand slams in a single game.

98.

In 1876, Ross Barnes hit the first-ever National League home run.

99.

Before the live-ball era, inside-the-park home runs were a lot more common than out-of-the-park home runs.

100.

Improvements in manufacturing technology made the balls travel further in the live-ball era.

101.

The shrinking size of the outfield also contributed to this increase in out-of-the-park home runs.

102.

Before 1931, a fair ball that bounced over an outfield fence was awarded as a home run.

103.

These were known as 'bounce home runs.'

104.

A lead-off home run is a home run hit by a team's first batter.

105.

Rickey Henderson holds the MLB record for the most lead-off home runs (81).

106.

Crag Biggio holds the record for the most National League lead-off home runs (53).

107.

A walk-off home run is scored when a home run ends the game.

108.

Two World Series have ended with a walk-off home run.

109.

The first was in 1960 when Bill Mazeroski hit one for the Pittsburgh Steelers.

110.

The second came in the 1993 World Series when Joe Carter hit a walk-off home run for the Toronto Blue Jays.

111.

Walk-off home runs are also called 'sudden death' or 'sudden victory' home runs.

112.

A back-to-back home run is when a home run is hit by two batters in a row.

113.

When three batters hit home runs in a row, it is known as a 'back-to-back-to-back' home run.

114.

Four home runs have been hit in a row only 11 times in MLB history.

115.

Hitting four home runs in a row is known as a 'back-to-back-to-back-to-back' home run.

116.

Only twice in MLB history have two brothers hit back-to-back home runs.

117.

These were the Waner brothers (1938) and the Upton brothers (2013).

118.

Ken Griffey Sr. and Ken Griffey Jr. are the only father-and-son duo to hit back-to-back home runs.

119.

No player in MLB history has hit five home runs in one game.

120.
In 2008, Gary Sheffield hit the 250,000th home run in MLB history.

121.
Outside of the MLB, the record for the most career home runs is held by Sadaharu Oh (868).

122.
Babe Ruth hit 60 home runs during the 1927 season.

123.
Aaron Judge hit 62 home runs in the 2022 season.

124.

In 1921, Babe Ruth hit a 575-foot home run.

125.

This is the furthest recorded home run in MLB history.

126.

However, many people believe it was further than 600 feet due to old measuring tools being inaccurate.

127.

In the same year (1921), Babe Ruth hit at least one 500-foot home run in all eight American League cities.

128.

Henry Chadwick is known as the 'Father of Baseball.'

129.

This is due to the number of stats he introduced to the game that are still used today.

130.

Despite baseball being a sport dominated by the US, Henry Chadwick was born in England.

131.

Statistics weren't a big part of baseball until the 1920s.

132.

The statistical and analytical study of baseball is known as 'sabermetrics.'

133.

The term was created by Bill James around 1980.

134.

The name sabermetrics comes from the Society for American Baseball Research (SABR).

135.

Morris Cohen (1919), referred to baseball as 'the national religion of the US.'

136.

In 1876, a National League ticket would cost 50 cents.

137.

Despite seeming cheap, 50 cents to watch a baseball match was a lot of money at the time.

138.

Baseball was therefore considered a middle-class sport.

139.

However, as other sports with higher ticket prices grew in popularity (football, basketball, etc.), baseball became more of a working-class game.

140.

A 2006 poll revealed that almost half of the US population considered themselves a baseball fan.

141.

However, only 9% said it was their favorite sport (football was 37%).

142.

In 2008, MLB set a record revenue of $6.5 billion.

143.

This was the first time in decades that the MLB revenue matched the NFL.

144.

In 2011, 95% of Venezuelans considered baseball to be their national sport.

145.

Baseball is also hugely popular in the Dominican Republic.

146.

Many of MLB's foreign players come from the Dominican Republic.

147.

83 of the 868 players in the 2017 MLB Opening Day rosters were from the Dominican Republic.

148.

Puerto Rico is another huge source of foreign talent for MLB.

149.

Roberto Clemente (Hall-of-Famer) is from Puerto Rico and is considered a national hero.

150.

Baseball is the national sport of Cuba.

151.

Baseball is also a very popular sport in Asia, especially in Japan and South Korea.

152.

Baseball is Japan's most popular spectator sport.

153.

Baseball was introduced to Japan as a school sport in 1872 and the first professional league was formed in 1936.

154.

Nippon Professional Baseball (NPB) is the highest level of baseball in Japan.

155.

The NPB consists of two leagues, the Pacific League and the Central League.

156.

There are six teams in the Pacific League and six teams in the Central League.

157.

However, before 1950, all teams played in the same league.

158.

Baseball is commonly called 'Yakyu' in Japanese.

159.

Horace Wilson (American) is responsible for introducing baseball to Japan.

160.

The popularity of baseball in Japan exploded in 1934.

161.

This was due to the Greater Japan Tokyo Baseball Club which was a team of all-stars created by Matsutaro Shoriki.

162.

Matsutaro Shoriki was a politician and also a huge baseball fan.

163.

Shoriki is known as 'the father of Japanese professional baseball.'

164.

Just like high school football is popular in the US, high school baseball is popular in Japan.

165.

Similarly to MLB, baseball in Japan has a farm system with two minor-leagues.

166.

These are the Eastern League and the Western League.

167.

The Eastern League is owned by the Central League and the Western League is owned by the Pacific League.

168.

The playing fields in the Nippon league (Japan) are also smaller.

169.

Five Nippon league fields are so small that they wouldn't be accepted in MLB.

170.

In 2011, NPB (Nippon Professional Baseball) limited games to three hours and thirty minutes.

171.

This is because a tsunami in 2011 imposed power limits in the stadiums.

172.

NPB teams have 28-player rosters compared to MLB's 26.

173.

Baseball is played in more than 75 countries around the world.

174.

Josh Gibson has the highest batting average in MLB history (0.372)

175.

Peter Rose holds the MLB record for the most singles (3,215).

176.

Alex Rodriguez has more MLB grand slams than any other player (25).

177.

Tommy Brown was just 17 years and 349 days old when he hit his first MLB home run.

178.

The MLB All-Star Game is a game between players from the American League and the National League.

179.

It is also known as the 'Midsummer Classic.'

180.
In this game, pitchers are selected by managers and starting fielders are picked by the fans.

181.
The All-Star Game is typically played on the second or third Tuesday in July.

182.
There wasn't an All-Star Game in 1945, nor in 2020.

183.
The 1945 game was cancelled due to World War II.

184.

The 2020 game was cancelled due to the COVID-19 pandemic.

185.

The first All-Star Game took place on July 6, 1933.

186.

The game was played at Comiskey Park in Chicago.

187.

The All-Star Game is now played every year, but it was originally only supposed to be a one-off event.

188.
Two All-Star Games were held each season between 1959 and 1962.

189.
The idea behind this was to make sure more money would go to the players' pension fund.

190.
After 1962, the event owners agreed to pay the players more money and it went back to being a once-a-year event.

191.
More than 2,000 players have played in the MLB All-Star Game.

192.

The venue for the All-Star Game changes every year and is decided by MLB.

193.

New York City has hosted more All-Star Games than any other city.

194.

Despite this, the New York Mets didn't host a game for 48 seasons between 1965 and 2012.

195.

The All-Star Game venue alternates between American and National Leagues every year.

196.

An American League (AL) team hosts the game in every year that ends in an odd number.

197.

A National League (NL) team hosts the game in every year that ends in an even number.

198.

However, this tradition has been broken a number of times.

199.

The first time was in 1951 when the Detroit Tigers (AL) hosted it as part of the city's 250th birthday.

200.

The Northern League hosted four games in a row between 2015 and 2018.

201.

In 2003, Dusty Baker managed the National League team despite recently moving to an American League team.

202.

The American League won the first-ever All-Star game 4-2.

203.

In the first All-Star game, the roster size for each league was 18.

204.

In 1934, the roster size increased to 20 players and then to 25 players in 1939.

205.

The roster size increased to 30 players in 1982, 32 players in 2003, and 33 players in 2009.

206.

Fans traditionally vote for the starting positions of players through ballots that are handed out at MLB games.

207.

As of 2022, fans vote for the chosen hitter on both teams.

208.

During the All-Star game, players wear the uniform of their current MLB team.

209.

However, in the first-ever All-Star Game, the National League team wore a grey uniform.

210.

As All-Star Game voting moved online, people began to cheat by voting multiple times.

211.

In 1999, a Red Sox fan voted for Nomar Garciaparra more than 39,000 times.

212.

A designated hitter was allowed in the All-Star Game for the first time in 1989.

213.

The All-Star Game MVP Award was first introduced in 1962.

214.

The award was originally called the 'Arch Ward Memorial Award.'

215.

This was named after Arch Ward, who created the concept of the All-Star Game.

216.

In 1970, the name of the award was changed to the 'Commissioner's Trophy.'

217.

Since 2002, the award has officially been known as 'The Ted Williams Most Valuable Player Award.'

218.

This honors the former Boston Red Sox player Ted Williams, who sadly passed away in 2002.

219.

The first tie in an All-Star Game occurred on July 31, 1961.

220.

Between 1933 and 1949, the American League won 12 of the first 16 All-Star Games.

221.

However, between 1950 and 1987, the National League won 33 of the 42 games.

222.

This streak included 19 wins out of 20 between 1963 and 1982.

223.

Since 1988, the American League has dominated, including a 13-game unbeaten streak between 1997 and 2009.

224.

The longest All-Star Game took place in 2008 and lasted four hours and fifty minutes.

225.

The Home Run Derby is a contest that is held the day before the All-Star Game.

226.

During this contest, many different players compete to see who can hit the most home runs.

227.

The first-ever Home Run Derby took place in 1985.

228.
The National Baseball Hall of Fame honors players, managers and other greats of baseball.

229.
The Hall of Fame was first established in 1936, but officially introduced in 1939 by Stephen Carlton Clark.

230.
The Hall of Fame museum is located in Cooperstown, New York.

231.
It was originally created to bring tourists to the area during the Great Depression.

232.

The first five men were elected into the Hall of Fame in 1936.

233.

These five were: Ty Cobb, Babe Ruth, Honus Wagner, Christy Mathewson and Walter Johnson.

234.

These five were officially inducted along with 20 others at the opening of the Hall in 1939.

235.

There are currently more than 340 people elected in the Hall of Fame.

236.

Adrian Beltre, Todd Helton, Jim Leyland and Joe Mauer were all elected in 2024.

237.

To be inducted into the Hall of Fame, players are either elected by the Baseball Writers' Association of America (BBWAA) or the Veterans Committee.

238.

The Veterans Committee is simply a name for the various committees of the National Baseball Hall of Fame Museum.

239.
Pete Rose and Joseph Jackson are ineligible to be inducted into the Hall of Fame.

240.
This is because they were banned from MLB for life after betting on their own teams.

241.
Jackson was banned after accepting a payment to purposely lose the 1919 World Series.

242.
Players have to choose the 'primary team' they are associated to when they are inducted.

243.

Each player has a photo taken with a cap on when they are inducted.

244.

Despite potentially playing for multiple teams, each player can only have one logo on their hat.

245.

Since 2001, the logo has been selected by the Hall of Fame, not the player.

246.

The Hall of Fame chooses the logo of the team where that player made their biggest mark.

247.

Before 2001, when players had played for multiple teams, they were able to choose which logo appeared on their cap.

248.

Frank Robinson chose to have a Baltimore Orioles cap despite playing ten seasons for the Cincinnati Reds.

249.

This was because he was a lot more successful at the Orioles.

250.

When Catfish Hunter was elected in 1987, he chose not to have any logo on his cap.

251.

Hunter played for the NY Yankees and Oakland Athletics and didn't want to disrespect either of them by choosing the other team's logo.

252.

The rule changed in 2001 due to rumors that teams were paying players to choose their logos.

253.

The Hall of Fame Museum attracts over 250,000 visitors every year.

254.

More than 17 million people have visited since it opened.

255.
There are more than 140,000 baseball cards in the Hall of Fame Museum.

256.
Willie Mays is regarded as one of the best baseball players ever and played 23 seasons in MLB.

257.
Mays hit 660 MLB home runs and appeared in 24 All-Star Games.

258.
He averaged 40 home runs per season between 1954 and 1966 and won 12 Gold Gloves.

259.
Ty Cobb holds the record for the most MLB batting titles (12).

260.
Cobb played 24 seasons in MLB, meaning that he won a batting title every two years.

261.
He is also credited with setting 9,000 MLB records during his career.

262.
Cobb's career success led to him being nicknamed 'The Georgia Peach.'

263.

Little League Baseball (LLB) is an organization that organizes youth baseball and softball leagues in the US.

264.

There are more than 180,000 teams and 2.6 million players in Little League Baseball

265.

This makes it the largest organized youth sports organization in the world.

266.

Just like in MLB, LLB has its own World Series.

267.

The LLB World Series is an annual tournament held in South Williamsport, Pennsylvania.

268.

The tournament was first held in 1947 and was originally called the 'National Little League Tournament.'

269.

Originally, only two teams from the US competed in the Series.

270.

Over 70 years later, the tournament is now worldwide and hosts 20 teams.

271.

On average, between 90 and 120 baseballs are used during an MLB game.

272.

Between 1969 and 1991, teams from Taiwan won 15 out of the 23 Series.

273.

In more recent times, Japanese teams have dominated, winning five of the seven series between 2010 and 2017.

274.

Overall though, teams from the US have won most of the tournaments.

275.

The LLB World Series is always held in August.

276.

The teams competing in the LLB World Series are made up of All-Star teams from each league.

277.

The LLB World Series is hosted in two stadiums: The Lamade Stadium and The Little League Volunteer Stadium.

278.

The Little League Volunteer Stadium was built in 2001 due to the growth of the LLB World Series.

279.

The LLB World Series is only for kids aged 10-12.

280.

Although the participation in the tournament is dominated by boys, more than 20 girls have played too.

281.

Victoria Roche was the first girl to compete in the tournament.

282.

In 2024, Lake Mary, Florida became the first team from Florida to win the LLB World Series.

283.

Hank Aaron's 755th home run baseball was sold at an auction for $650,000.

284.

Although the participation in the tournament is dominated by boys, more than 20 girls have played too.

285.

Victoria Roche was the first girl to compete in the tournament.

286.

In 2024, Lake Mary, Flordia became the first team from Florida to win the LLB World Series.

287.

California is the most successful state when it comes to LLB World Series wins.

288.

As of 2024, they have won 8 titles (20% of all US titles).

289.

Joe McCarthy is regarded by many as being the best baseball manager of all time.

290.

He was the first manager to win pennants with both American League and National League teams.

291.

In total, McCarthy won nine pennants and seven World Series as a manager.

292.

Connie Mack holds the record for the most MLB wins as a manager (3,731).

293.

Despite this, he also holds the record for the most losses and the most ties.

294.

In total, Connie Mack managed more than 7,000 MLB games in his career.

295.

Vic Harris holds the record for the highest win percentage as a manager (66.3%).

296.

Despite this record, Vic Harris has not been inducted into the Hall of Fame.

297.

The highest all-time MLB attendance was recorded on March 29, 2008, in a preseason game between Boston Red Sox and LA Dodgers.

298.

115,300 people attended the game.

299.

According to the Hall of Fame, this is the only game where over 100,000 people have definitively attended.

300.

The lowest MLB attendance was recorded in 1882 during a game between Troy Trojans and the Worcesters. Only six people turned up to watch.

Made in United States
North Haven, CT
17 December 2024

62675779R00046